Sisters in Christ

Belinda L. Davis

Sisters in Christ

Titus 2 - Women of God

Bible Study

Belinda L. Davis

Belinda L. Davis

Copyright © 2025 by Belinda L. Davis:
First Edition, 2025
Published in the United States of America

ISBN: 979-8-218-72099-5

Dedications

I dedicate this Bible Study to every person that has ever taught the Word of God in any capacity. Thank you for your hard work and dedication to the craft of diving into the Lord's most precious Word. May God give you all that your heart has desired.

To my church family, Macedonia Baptist Church and Pastor Terry and First Lady Theresa Minor, Sr., thank you for your love and encouragement throughout the years. May God give you many more fruitful years working in His vineyard. To Pastor Emeritus Charles and First Lady Lorraine Twymon, Jr., thank you for your love, support, and spirit of excellence for God's work.

To my family, I am grateful for your love and support. Writing this Bible Study took me longer than I had hoped, but it is now complete. To my Mother-in-love Joyce, thank you for raising the Man of God that I love so much to fear the Lord and to live for Him. To my sisters, Shelia, Dorie, Ardette (Sylvester), and Sherry, thank you for always being there for me all my life with a word of encouragement and always showing me love. To my brother Ferman (Linda), you are the epitome of what living a

Godly lifestyle looks like. Thank you for always giving me good advice and an example of how to say yes to God.

To Iron Sharpens Iron Ministries, you Ladies know how God has moved on our behalf over the years. Thank you for your diligence to uphold the Blood-Stained Banner by praying weekly for our family, friends, nation, and the world. Thank you for keeping the many conversations and me sharing my heart with you over the years confident (everything should not be shared). Your love and support are greatly appreciated.

To the Ladies that stood with me on my Wedding Day, better known as my Bridal Party, I thank you for covering me over the years with prayer and love. May God Bless each of you for your dedication to living for Him. Angela, Tiffany, Ashley, and Sherry, I will always be grateful for your encouragement, kindness, love, and support over the years.

To my husband Brian, you have always been my rock, my love, and my protector. Only we know how God has changed our lives and kept this union on track for these 20 years of marriage. Thank you for being you, every day and always. I am grateful for you and love you endlessly.

Table of Contents

Belinda L. Davis

Introduction

You determine how much you grow in your Christian journey. Out of all the religions of the world, Christianity is the only one where being all you can be is just enough to get you through the day but not enough to get you through tomorrow. We need Daily Prayer with God to make it! Just like we eat every day and breathe every day we need to commune with the Lord, every day. I have found in my 5 decades of life that being a Christian is more than what our words say. It is living this thing out. It is praying for yourself that you don't pop off on your enemies when provoked. It is really learning to lean and depend on God to handle the things He wants us to give to Him. Just give it to Him, and Let It Go! It is really living out the Love thy Neighbor stuff, really!

It is forgiving that person at work that knows you are a Christian but still talks badly about your faith or makes fun of your faith and you must look the other way. It is keeping your eyes on Jesus when your strength is at its end, and you have already given up. It is looking at yourself in the mirror again and admitting, yeah, I blew it and asking God for forgiveness. Yes, being a Christian is hard work that pays off often when we least expect it. God sees it even if man doesn't care to even look. God sees it even when we think we are all alone, never. God knows our hearts even when we think it's too late, Trust Him. This Bible Study will challenge you, Sister. You will think, reflect, cry, pray, and prayerfully grow from this Bible Study. So, get your Bible, put on your game face, and dive deep into the Word.

Your Sister in Christ,

Belinda

How to Use this Bible Study

For each chapter of this Bible Study, there is a scripture, and the focus will be on the underlined portion of the scripture. My suggestion is to have your Bible ready and look each scripture up and even look at various translations. Also, you may consider investing into a good Women's Study Bible that has great notes and references to help you dive deeper into the Word.

I love creative writing, so I decided to add a "Scenario" section which has interactions between two characters. Character 1: Sis Suzie - A retired 64-year-old educator, Wife, Mom, and Grandmother who has been running for Jesus a long time. Character 2: Sis Wonita - A 31-year-old Single Mom, dating, and a Babe in Christ (less than 2 years) with a 4-year-old Son Bobby whose dad is in and out of their lives. We will consider the various situations they find themselves in and how you would handle them if it were you.

The "Deep Dive" section will have questions to ponder about the chapter at hand. I have left plenty of room for notes and areas to answer questions. Just below Deep Dive is the "More Please" section. This is where you get to look up scriptures and answer a few questions all with the hope of stirring up the Gift within you. If you find some of the questions challenging, I have put "Answers to More Please Questions" at the end of the book to stir up some thoughts on the text. These are just suggestions to hopefully point you in the right direction.

3 The aged women likewise, that they be in behaviour as becometh holiness, not false accusers, not given to much wine, teachers of good things;
4 That they may teach the young women to be sober, to love their husbands, to love their children,
5 To be discreet, chaste, keepers at home, good, obedient to their own husbands, that the word of God be not blasphemed.

Titus 2:3-5 KJV

Belinda L. Davis

Chapter 1 – Character Matters

Titus 2:3 KJV

The aged women likewise, that they be in <u>behaviour as becometh</u> <u>holiness</u>, not false accusers, not given to much wine, teachers of good things;

Do you know that the Holy Spirit lives in your Body (I Cor 6:29)? As Sisters in Christ, we are called to live holy lifestyles. What does this look like? We see in Titus 2:3, Paul tells Titus to teach the older women in his church community to "be in behaviour as becometh holiness". Some translations use the phrase "Reverent in Behavior." This means to take the office of a Woman of God seriously. We are to live our lives consecrated unto God. This speaks to how we carry ourselves, our character.

Are you the one that wears very revealing clothing to work? Are you the one that's quick to not only give your enemy a piece of your mind but also your fist? These may seem like small things, but God wants us to live for Him in all areas of our lives. No matter what area you are struggling in, give it to God, ask for forgiveness, and press on. Living a consecrated life takes work and yielding to the Holy Spirit. We have work to do. Let's Go!

Scenario: Sis Suzie pulled into the grocery store parking lot and heard this loud curse filled song coming from the car directly next to her. As the vehicle was pulling off, to her shock and surprise, it was Sis Wonita from church. What should Sis Suzie say to Sis Wonita when she sees her at Bible Study tonight?

Deep Dive

Look up the definition of Behavior and write it down.

Give an example of a time in your life where you had to change your behavior to fit in?

More Please – Look up the following scriptures.

1. I Tim 4:7 NIV. What are we told to have "nothing to do with"?

2. I Tim 5:1-2 NIV. How should we treat older and younger women?

3. Col 3:12 NIV. What should we "clothe" ourselves with?

4. I Cor 10:31 NIV. What can we as Sisters in Christ do to the Glory of God?

If we are eager to change our behavior for school, work, or even in our family gatherings, how much more should we be willing to yield to God in our behavior?

You did great! Now let's move over to Chapter 2.

Prayer

Father God in the Name of Jesus we ask You to forgive us for those areas that we have missed the mark in our walk with You. For this we apologize. We ask You to help us see ourselves the way You see us. We have been fearfully and wonderfully made in Your image. We find our identity in You Lord. May we grow in Your Word which will help us to live as You would have us to live. May we grow in grace and in the knowledge of You Lord Jesus. Please help us Lord to be the Women You have called us to be in this hour. In Jesus' Name we pray, Amen.

Chapter 2 – Don't Do the Devils Work!

Titus 2:3 KJV

The aged women likewise, that they be in behaviour as becometh holiness, <u>not false accusers</u>, not given to much wine, teachers of good things;

As we look at the next thing Paul tells Titus, we see "not false accusers" listed. Some translations use the term "not slanderers". So, what is a slanderer? This is someone that spreads malicious gossip. The Greek word for "false accuser" is the same word used for the devil. Far too often people's reputations and even their livelihoods have been ruined by this type of activity and sadly, even the Church has fallen victim to this. Whenever we share or even listen to gossip, we are doing the devil's work. How can I say that? Jesus used this same word when describing the Devil in Matt 4 when He was tested in the wilderness. Moving forward, let's repent of this activity and remove it from our lives all together. We, as Sisters in Christ, are commanded to love our enemies and pray for those that persecute us (Matt 5: 44).

It's in our nature to want to get revenge when we are wronged. If we are cut off in traffic or if someone yells at us at work, we want to pay them back. And some juicy gossip is always one way to get pay back, but that is not what a Woman of God should engage in. It's easy to gossip, it's difficult to pray for your enemy. But that is the mark of a mature Christian. So, the next time someone comes to you with gossip, say "Let's Pray for them" and see how God moves.

Scenario: After Bible Study, Sis Suzie saw Sis Wonita heading toward the door to leave. Before she could reach her, Sis Patty was gossiping about what happened in the choir in the last rehearsal. Allegedly, one of the women in the choir is dating a married Man. What should Sis Suzie tell Sis Wonita about this "news"?

Deep Dive

Have you ever had someone gossip about you? How did it make you feel?

More Please – Look up the following scriptures.

1. I Tim 3:11 ESV. What are some of the qualities that a Deacon's wife should possess?

2. 2 Tim 3:1-5 ESV. What did Paul prophesy about the last days?

3. James 3:6 ESV. What did James say about the tongue?

4. Matt 4:3-4 ESV. What should we as Women of God say when the devil tries to tempt us?

Since many of us know the pain and confusion gossip has caused in our own lives, we should be just that concerned when it is done to others.

Let's keep going! On to Chapter 3.

Prayer

Father God in the Name of Jesus we come to You asking that you forgive us where we have fallen short especially in and around gossip and spreading rumors. Help us to be more compassionate realizing it could be us who are the subject of such mean speech. May we always remember that we should use our words to encourage and not teardown someone else. In Jesus' Name we pray, Amen.

Chapter 3 – Clean and Sober

Titus 2:3 KJV

The aged women likewise, that they be in behaviour as becometh holiness, not false accusers, <u>not given to much wine,</u> teachers of good things;

The older women during Paul's day in the Roman and Greek culture would often indulge in gossip and "much wine". Unfortunately, these are still devices that the enemy knows he can trap us in if we are not careful. The Center for Disease Control gives guidance that women should consume no more than one alcoholic drink a day. They also recommend that if you are recovering from alcohol addiction, you should avoid it all together. What about those that are not addicted but just want a glass of wine every now and then? It may not do much harm if it's a special occasion. Yet, even then you must still only consume one drink, just one! This goes against everything in our culture today but as Women of God we have a duty to love ourselves and others.

Some of you may have already been negatively impacted by alcoholism, maybe a parent, your spouse, family members, or even friends may have tried with no success to fight off the addiction. Maybe wine is not your vice. Maybe it's too much fast food, or too much sugar, or too much toxic tv, or maybe it's the ding of your cell phone. Anything that takes our minds away from the Lord, can become an addiction. Remember God is a jealous God (Ex 34:14). He wants all of you, heart, soul, mind, and strength (Mark 12:30). Keep praying for the Lord's help to live for Him. Keep holding on to God. He will see you through.

Scenario: Sis Suzie finally has an opportunity to talk with Sis Wonita. During the conversation, she shared that her father was a recovering alcoholic, but she likes to drink a little cognac at family gatherings. What should Sis Suzie say to Sis Wonita, if anything?

Deep Dive

Have you ever struggled with an addiction? Did anyone try to help you to overcome it? What was your response when others tried to help you?

More Please – Look up the following scriptures.

1. Rom 6:6,14 NLT. How does Paul illustrate our old and new lives in Christ?

2. Gal 4:3,7 NLT. How does Paul describe a life before and after giving their lives to Jesus?

3. I Thess 5:6-8 NLT. How should we prepare for the Lord's return?

4. 2 Pet 2:19 NLT. What are signs of a false teacher?

Living counterculture may seem like you are missing out on the fun stuff. But living for the Lord yields dividends now and in eternity. Let's keep going! On to Chapter 4.

Prayer

Father God in the name of Jesus we come before You to say thank You. Thank You Lord for giving us another opportunity to get it right today. Thank You for the love you have shown us all our lives even when we didn't know You. Lord, please help us as we strive to live out this Christian journey. May we always remember that You hear us when we pray even in times of weakness. Please forgive us, just as our Lord Jesus Christ has said, as we forgive others. Thank you, Lord, for Your Grace and Your Mercy. In Jesus' name, Amen.

Chapter 4 – Teach the Right Stuff

Titus 2:3 KJV

The aged women likewise, that they be in behaviour as becometh holiness, not false accusers, not given to much wine, <u>teachers of good things</u>;

A fun fact about this portion of Paul's instructions to Titus is that this phrase only appears this one time in scripture. Why is it important that women are taught "good things"? Far too often in our society, we are bombarded with negative and ungodly images of ourselves and our faith. We as Women of God must counter these images with what the Word of God tells us. As stated in Prov 31: 26 speaking with kindness is a good thing. Loving your neighbor as yourself is a good thing (Matt 22:39). Seeking good and not evil is a good thing (Amos 5:14). Praising and worshiping the Lord is a good thing (Ps 100:1-2). Yes, teaching the Word of God is a good thing because the Word is right (Ps 33:4).

Living a life for Jesus in a time when our faith is mocked may be difficult, but we are called for such a time as this. God did not give us a spirit of fear, but of love, power, and a sound-mind (2

Tim 1:7). Remember what our Lord told us, we must love God with all our heart, soul, mind, and strength and love your neighbors as yourself (Mark 12:30-31).

Scenario: Sis Suzie invited Sis Wonita over to her house for a game night with her family. Sis Wonita doesn't have family nearby, so the invite was a welcomed change for her. While at Sis Suzie's house, she noticed the many scriptures in poster frames on her walls. Sis Wonita had some questions about the scriptures.

Deep Dive

Do you have a bible out or scriptures in plain view when visitors come to your home? What are some good things that you have taught someone about the Lord?

More Please – Look up the following scriptures.

1. Ps 119:65-68 ESV. What and Who does the Psalmist say are good?

2. John 20:16 ESV. What did Mary call Jesus in Aramaic?

3. Jer 9:20 ESV. What did Jeramiah tell the women to do?

Being a teacher of good things in a world that glamorizes the profane may seem like a difficult task. However, with God's help, we can share our experiences as well as our testimonies all to the Glory of God. Now, on to Chapter 5.

Prayer

Father God in the name of Jesus, we come before You to say thank You for all You do for us. May we learn from Your Word all that we need to be able to rightly divide the Word of Truth (2 Tim 2:15). May we continue to grow in grace and the knowledge of our Lord Jesus Christ. In Jesus' Name We Pray, Amen.

Chapter 5 – Love Matters

Titus 2:4 KJV

That they may teach the young women <u>to be sober</u>, <u>to love their husbands</u>, <u>to love their children</u>,

During the time of Paul's writing to Titus, the Cretan society allowed marriage from puberty to late teenage years. So, training a young soon-to-be-bride about loving her husband and children was important. Most newer translations omit "to be sober" and just use "train" or "encourage". I found it interesting to think that you would have to train or even encourage a wife and mom to love her husband and her children, however, it is needed. Just as in the Biblical days, young women should be trained or encouraged to love their husbands and their children. So, what does that look like? For loving your husband, there is a book called *5 Love Languages* by Gary Chapman that I would recommend married couples and anyone considering getting married to read. It has been a help and blessing for me and my husband as we approach 20 years of marriage ourselves.

Regarding loving your children, although I am not a mother of human babies, I do have fur babies and they have taught me how to love as a parent. I also have many childhood memories of being shown love by my mother, who is now in Heaven. I was shown love by having food, shelter, clean clothes, to name a few, and more toys than I deserved. I was also disciplined when I needed. Showing your children love, teaching them to be good citizens, and teaching them about the Lord is all a part of being a loving Mom. May the Lord give you wisdom in this area.

Scenario: Sis Suzie and Sis Wonita decided to go to a restaurant after church with some choir members. Sis Suzie began sharing how she prepared a surprise retirement party for her husband with the help of her children. She also shared how she spent her days off with her children at the museum and spent time at the local park when they were little.

Deep Dive

Read Proverbs 31:28. What does this Virtuous Woman's Husband and children do to her? What is something memorable that your family has done for you?

More Please – Look up the following scriptures.

1. I Tim 5:14 NIV. Why did Paul encourage the young widows to remarry?

2. I John 3:14 NIV. How do we know that we have "passed from death to life"?

3. Prov 22:6 NIV. What are parents to do for their children?

Being Sisters in Christ, we should not only show love to our husbands and children, but also to our neighbors. Let's keep going! On to Chapter 6.

Prayer

Father God in the name of Jesus, may we always remember that Your love is great toward us. It is unsearchable. Please help us to love others, especially when it comes to our families. May we have wisdom on when to speak and how to respond in all areas of our lives. May we be slow to speak and quick to forgive when difficulties arise. Help us to love like You love Lord. In Jesus' name, Amen.

Chapter 6 – Control Yourself

Titus 2:5 KJV

To be <u>discreet</u>, chaste, keepers at home, good, obedient to their own husbands, that the word of God be not blasphemed.

Being discreet here means to curb one's desires or impulses. Some translations will say "self-controlled" or "sound-mind". Paul wanted Titus to teach the older women that they should remind the younger women that being discreet will set them apart from the other women in their society. We today should be discreet, having self-control is a needed characteristic today. Being able to say what is on your mind can be a good thing only if you are not having a curse filled tirade at the same time. How do we live a discreet life today? We trust God to keep us and not worry and stress ourselves out thinking about "what could happen" (Prov 3:5-6). When layoffs happen on the job, we rest knowing that God is our Source, and the job is just a resource. Being discreet also involves not letting people get under your skin or control your emotions. I have learned that once a person gets you to think about them long after the argument is over, they win.

Let's put being discreet into practice this week. The next time you are challenged online with an offensive post or comment, LET IT GO! Pray for the person and watch the Lord work on them and you.

Scenario: Sis Suzie was at choir rehearsal when Sis Wonita came in and sat down. She was upset about the back and forth that was happening on social media between her and her old friend Monica. Monica was spreading a rumor about Sis Wonita and they were in a heated post about it. Most of the choir members had already seen the post so it was no surprise that Sis Wonita was upset. What should Sis Suzie say to Sis Wonita?

Deep Dive

Has someone offended you on social media, email, or via text message? How did you respond to the person? What did you learn from that experience?

More Please – Look up the following scriptures.

1. Prov 2:11 NIV. What will discretion do for you?

2. Acts 9:36 NIV. Who was Tabitha (Dorcas)?

3. I Tim 5:10 NIV. What are some of the good works that we as Women of God should do?

Living a discreet lifestyle as a Woman of God can help us to grow in our faith as we navigate the many tests and trials of life. You are doing great! Now on to Chapter 7!

Prayer

Father God in the name of Jesus, I come to You asking for your help today. Help me Lord to be discreet. To curb any and all appetites that are keeping me from growing in your will and your way. Help me God, when I am challenged by someone, to not say everything that comes to mind. Help me to be quick to forgive so that my prayers are not hindered. Also, Lord, when possible, may I be willing and ready to reconcile with the person. Thank You Lord in advance. In Jesus' name, Amen.

Chapter 7 – Clean on the Inside

Titus 2:5 KJV

To be discreet, <u>chaste</u>, keepers at home, good, obedient to their own husbands, that the word of God be not blasphemed.

Here in Titus 2:5, the King James version uses the word "chaste" which can also mean "pure". The older women were to also teach the younger women how valuable their chastity or their virginity is before God. Physical relations before marriage were very frowned upon in the days of Paul and Titus. Often, even if a woman were raped, she would remain unmarried because they were seen as no longer chaste (tragic story of Tamar in 2 Sam 13:1-20). Since women in that day were unable to care for themselves financially it was very important to marry and raise a family. Women that did not marry had to live with their parents or often a male relative.

Today, a woman's virginity is not as valued in the eyes of men anymore. I have even heard men say, "How can you know if you are compatible if you don't experience one another before marriage?" That is a lie from the devil. God's word is still true! He wants the very best for you, my Sister. Not heartbreak, disease, unplanned pregnancy, or a life full of disappointments.

He has a plan to prosper you and give you a future (Jer 29:11). He wants you to prosper and be in good health as your soul prospers (3 John 1:2). He loves you with an everlasting love (Jer 31:3).

Being chaste is a part of that. If you have missed the mark in this area of your walk, confess it to the Lord, repent, and keep moving! If you are currently in an ungodly relationship that is robbing you of your full potential in God, cut the cord! You may hurt now, but God will hold you up and sustain you if you ask Him to. Presenting our bodies to God as a living sacrifice, holy, and acceptable unto Him is what He requires from us (Rom 12:1). So, pick yourself up, dust yourself off, put God first, and keep pushin'.

Scenario: Sis Wonita called Sis Suzie on the phone to talk to her about her relationship with her son Bobby's Father, Pete. Although they share a son together, they do not have a good relationship. Sometimes she spends the night at Pete's house only to get into an argument the next morning. What advice should Sis Suzie give Sis Wonita?

Deep Dive

Do you think virginity is valued in today's society?

More Please – Look up the following scriptures.

1. I Cor 6:15, 18 ESV. What are our bodies members of? What sin is against one's own body?

2. 2 Cor 11:2 ESV. How did Paul say he presented the Corinthians to Christ?

3. John 4:17-18, 28-29 ESV. How many "husbands" did the Woman at the well say she had? What did she tell the people from her homeland?

In our fast-paced society, living for today is all the rage. We as Women of God have a higher standard, God's standard, that we must live by. Let us hold fast to our profession of faith and not waiver. Great job! On to Chapter 8!

Prayer

Father God in the name of Jesus, we come before You to say, Thank You. Thank You God for not allowing us to die in our sins. Thank You God for forgiving us when we fell short of Your perfect plan for our lives. Thank You Lord for your grace and your mercy. Most of all, thank You Lord for salvation for without it we are eternally lost. Please forgive us for missing the mark any time we failed to use discretion with these temples You have given us Lord. May we live our lives moving forward in a way that give You glory. In Jesus' name we pray, Amen.

Chapter 8 – Making a House a Home

Titus 2:5 KJV

To be discreet, chaste, <u>keepers at home</u>, good, obedient to their own husbands, that the word of God be not blasphemed.

Ladies, as Women of God and Sister's in Christ, we must make sure that we keep our homes as if the Lord will stop by for a visit at any moment. I remember in the days when the Life Insurance man would stop by my childhood home. My Mom made sure to have the living room and dining room very clean and presentable. Some families even used to have a couch that had plastic on it and no one could sit on the couch, except guests. In the days of Paul and Titus, women took pride in how they kept their homes and made sure they were tidy and welcoming.

Today, we should do the same whether we are stay at home Moms, Single, Married, or just Women in various stages of our lives. Our homes should always be warm, inviting, and ready for fellowship. We should make sure we have peace in our homes. I would encourage you Sisters to have a Prayer Closet or at least a dedicated area in your home to pray. Having a privacy and quiet place in your home to seek God's face is needed for us Women of God.

When was the last time someone invited you over to their home? Better yet, when was the last time you invited someone over to spend time with you and your family that was not your family? It is my prayer that after this Bible Study, that we Sisters in Christ will stretch out of our comfort zones and show up when invited to someone's home or gathering as well as invite others to our homes. You never know how the Lord may use these encounters to draw someone to Christ. So, Ladies, let's be great keepers at home, showing love along the way, and just maybe we can win a soul or two for the Kingdom of God.

Scenario: Sis Helen invited the Women in choir to her home for a Girls Game Night. Sis Wonita and Sis Suzie were excited to attend. Each lady brought a dish and participated in the game selections. They had an enjoyable time together.

Deep Dive

When was the last time you invited a non-family member to your home? What was the occasion?

More Please – Look up the following scriptures.

1. Prov 31:27 NIV.   What does the Virtuous Woman do regarding her household?

2. Ps 128:3 NIV. How is the wife described by the Psalmist?

3. I Tim 5:13-14 NIV. What are some of the pitfalls of being idle?

As busy Women of God, we have so much on our plates, but we should make sure that we are keeping our homes loving, inviting, and full of God's peace. Now, let's move on to Chapter 9!

Prayer

Father God in the name of Jesus, Lord, we thank You for a place to call home. We thank You for providing us with a safe place to lie our heads down at night. Thank You Lord for our neighbors, family, and friends. We thank You Lord for blessing us with earthly treasures. Lord help those that are not as friendly because of past hurts or that are alone. May we show others hospitality in our homes as we strive to grow in grace. In Jesus' name, Amen.

Chapter 9 – Good for Something

Titus 2:5 KJV

To be discreet, chaste, keepers at home, <u>good</u>, obedient to their own husbands, that the word of God be not blasphemed.

Just as in the days of Paul and Titus, today we should be good Women of God. Good here means in a moral sense. Other translations use the word "kind". What does that look like? Living a good moral lifestyle showing kindness to everyone we meet shows our growth in Christ. As a matter of fact, goodness is a Fruit of the Spirit (Gal 5:22). When we show kindness to someone that may not be so kind to us, we are showing our maturity in Christ. It is easy to do whatever our flesh wants us to do, it is hard to yield to the Spirit of God because our spirit is willing, but our flesh is weak (Mark 14:38).

To live a good life in this evil and wicked world is a hard road to follow. We are always seen by the world as weak, indifferent, and just out of touch when we stand on our morals and say "No" to the devil and the alluring traps that he sets. Even when we are tempted with evil, the Lord keeps us and provides us with a way to escape when we are tempted with evil (I Cor 10:13). This is where a good prayer life comes in. No matter what test or temptation we face, with prayer and keeping our eyes on Jesus, we can still live a good life. Are we perfect? No. Will we never sin again? No. Can we live a good Christ-centered life with all our flaws and shortcoming? Yes. My Sister, keep Jesus first, keep praying, and know that your living is not in vain. God has more for you. Keep pushin'!

Scenario: Sis Suzie was standing in line to pay for her groceries when a man cut in front of her. She told him politely that the line started behind her, but he said "I've got somewhere to be! You should have moved up!" The store manager noticed what had happened and opened another line and made sure Sis Suzie was in front. When asked by the store manager about the situation, Sis Suzie said "It's ok. I'll just pray for him."

Deep Dive

Has anyone treated you unkindly because of your faith? How did you handle that situation?

More Please – Look up the following scriptures.

1. I Tim 5:9-10 ESV. What were some of the characteristics Paul mentioned of widows in the church?

2. Ps 34:12-13 ESV. What did the Psalmist say you should do if you want to love life and see good days?

3. I Tim 5:25 CEV reads "It is the same with good deeds. Some are easily seen, but none of them can be hidden." What are some good deeds that you have done recently?

I recall in my youth; many people would say that someone that did a lot of bad things was "Good for Nothing." We, as Women of God, should always make sure that our faith is backed up with works, showing that we are Good for Something.

Great job! On to Chapter 10!

Prayer

Father God in the name of Jesus, help us to be more kind. Sometimes it's easier said than done, especially in our society today. May we look to You for guidance on when and where we should show kindness. Help us Lord to realize when we are missing the mark in this area. Thank You God for showing us kindness daily. In Jesus' name, Amen.

Chapter 10 – Obey Bae

Titus 2:5 KJV

To be discreet, chaste, keepers at home, good, <u>obedient to their own husbands</u>, that the word of God be not blasphemed.

Titus was to encourage the older women to teach the younger women to be obedient to their own husbands. Some translations use the term "subject" to their own husbands. What does this mean? The Greek word used here for obedient is hypotasso which means "to arrange under or be subordinate, submit one's control, to obey". Christian wives must understand God's order. The Lord made Adam first and then Eve. Since husbands are head of their wives, they are responsible for the family structure in God's eyes.

What does this look like? When there is a major decision to be made regarding family planning, moving, paying rent or mortgage, how to raise the children, and the like, the husband is to be directing or leading these vital decisions. Just like there is only one CEO of a company, so it is in the home. The husband is the "CEO of the home" per say. Yes, his wife can add input but the one responsible if things are going to go right or wrong is the husband.

In our modern society, being obedient to our bosses is a no brainer if we want to keep our jobs, but for many of us Ladies, being obedient to our husbands is disagreement waiting to happen. My prayer is that husbands and wives learn to improve their roles in the home to line up with God's Word. If you are struggling in this area, pray that the Lord helps you and your husband to follow His Will for your lives.

Scenario: Sis Suzie shared a story in her small group about how her and her husband were on the verge of divorce because she was not being obedient to him. She shared how her Pastor showed her scripture and prayed for them and how God worked in both of their hearts.

Deep Dive

Wives: Please share a time in your marriage when you obeyed your husband.

Singles: Please share a time when you had to obey your father, brother, or any male in authority.

More Please – Look up the following scriptures.

1. I Cor 11:3 NIV. How does Paul describe the relationship between the Husband, Wife, and Christ?

2. Luke 2:46-51 NIV. How did Jesus respond to Mary and Joseph after he was located at the temple? What can we learn from this?

3. Matt 10:30 NIV. God loves you so much my Sister. What does He keep a count of?

We live in a time when many marriages fail within the first few years. Others do not even consider marriage as an option. For those that want to be married someday, I encourage you to pray for your future Husband. Pray that God opens his eyes to not make foolish decisions that will hurt you in marriage. Pray that God keeps his heart and mind in all that he endeavors to do. Pray that he learns from his mistakes and keeps God first. For my married Sisters, along with the list already mentioned, pray that God crowns him with wisdom on next steps for the family.

Great job Ladies! On to Chapter 11!

Prayer

Father God in the name of Jesus, thank You Lord for giving us the opportunity to experience a glimpse of how Your Kingdom looks in the form of Marriage. For in Your Word, you said the Husband is the head of the Wife as Christ is the head of the Church. Lord, please bless each marriage that tries to live out Your Biblical worldview. Bless each wife as she tries to obey her husband. Bless each husband as he tries to listen to Your voice for direction for his family. Lord, please bless those that are Single and want to be married one day. May they seek Your face while they wait and still work in your vineyard. Lord, we also pray for those whose marriages failed. Please heal their hearts. Help all of us Lord to be obedient to You in all areas of our lives. In Jesus' name, Amen.

Chapter 11 – Watch Your Mouth

Titus 2:5 KJV

To be discreet, chaste, keepers at home, good, obedient to their own husbands, that <u>the word of God be not blasphemed.</u>

Finally, the reason why the young women were to be taught all these things was to make sure that the "Word of God be not blasphemed". The word blaspheme means to slander, to speak lightly or profanely of sacred things. Jesus gave us a warning that to blaspheme the Holy Spirit, there is no forgiveness for it (Matt 12:31). Today, we must make sure that we are standing on God's Word and that we are not falling for the devil's schemes to try to get us to believe his lies. We as Women of God have a duty to teach the truth of the Gospel, to live a life that shows we belong to God, and to love our neighbor as ourselves.

The Word of God tells us that out of the abundance of the heart the mouth speaks (Luke 6:45). Whatever is in your heart will come out at some point. That is why it is so important to Study God's Word so that we can know what is that good and perfect will that He has for us (Rom 12:2).

Scenario: Sis Suzie and Sis Wonita attended a Women's Conference and the guest Speaker talked about speaking the truth. She made a point to mention that it's not just what you say but how you say it that matters. It all should be done in love.

Deep Dive

Have you ever been in a situation where a person made fun of or had something mean to say about your faith? How did you handle that test?

More Please – Look up the following scriptures.

1. Luke 22:63-65 NIV. What were some of the wicked things that were done to Christ before His crucifixion?

2. 2 Pet 2:1-2 NIV. Who will many follow to 'swift destruction'?

3. I Pet 4:4 ESV. Why will the world speak evil of you?

Closing Thoughts and Prayer

It is my prayer that you have enjoyed this Women's Bible Study, and I hope this is a springboard for you to search the scriptures even more. All of us know a Sis Suzie and a Sis Wonita. Which one are you? Do you give advice and show support to others or are you the one looking for just a little help to get through? Either way, may you listen attentively for God's voice with any advice you receive and may you not be afraid or ashamed to ask for help. All of us more Seasoned Sisters are here with open arms, a listening ear, and a prayer.

Beautiful Ladies, let us pray for the younger women in our

churches, communities, and societies at large. There are so many vices and traps set for them by the enemy. May we stand in the gap for them that they are pulled out of the fire and into God's wonderful light. May we be examples of Women living for God that can show compassion, sympathy, and give a little grace when needed. May we use our words to encourage and not gossip and tear others down. May we let the light that was given to us shine in this dark world leading people directly to Jesus. I want to close this Bible Study with prayer.

Father God,

I come before you to say Thank You. Thank you for putting on my heart the idea for this Bible Study and providing the tools to do the research for every section of scripture. You are Awesome God, and I am forever grateful.

Please forgive us for falling short and missing the mark. We are sorry. Please Bless each Lady and her home, her family, and everyone connected to her. May she go on to dive into more of Your Holy Word that will help her grow closer to You Lord God.

May these Women of God learn to take everything to You in prayer, even the painful things that just won't go away. May they see growth in how they conduct themselves in society. May they show compassion to others that are not so kind or loving to them.

May they put down the bad habits that are against their health and wellbeing. May their husbands, children, family, and friends see a change in their lives that can only be attributed to You Lord God. May they see peace in their homes and a better prayer life. May they step out of their comfort zones and show love to this dying world.

Lord, we thank You for peace in the midst of storms, comfort in the midst of sorrow, faith in times of doubt, and love when fear rises up. May Your perfect will be done in each Woman's life. May we as Sisters in Christ grow in grace and faith in You Lord Jesus.

In Jesus' Name I pray, Amen.

Answers to More Please Questions

{these are only suggestions}

Chapter 1

1. I Tim 4:7 NIV. What are we told to have "nothing to do with"?

Answer: godless myths and old wives' tales

2. I Tim 5:1-2 NIV. How should we treat older and younger women?

Answer: older women as mothers, and younger women as sisters, with absolute purity.

3. Col 3:12 NIV. What should we "clothe" ourselves with?

Answer: clothe yourselves with compassion, kindness, humility, gentleness and patience.

4. Q: I Cor 10:31 NIV. What can we as Sisters in Christ do to the Glory of God?

Answer: whatever you do, do it all for the glory of God.

Chapter 2

1. I Tim 3:11 ESV. What are some of the qualities that a Deacon's wife should possess?

Answer: dignified, not slanderers, but sober-minded, faithful in all things.

2. 2 Tim 3:1-5 ESV. What did Paul prophesy about the last days?

Answer: People will become slanderous in the last days among many other ungodly things. And we are warned to avoid such people.

3. James 3:6 ESV. What did James say about the tongue?

Answer: The tongue is a fire. In other words, your tongue can contaminate your body if you are not careful.

4. Matt 4:3-4 ESV. What should we as Women of God say when the devil tries to tempt us?

Answer: Just as the Lord Jesus quoted scripture, we should too when temptation comes our way.

Chapter 3

1. Rom 6:6,14 NLT. How does Paul illustrate our old and new lives in Christ?

Answer: old sinful selves were crucified with Christ and we are no longer slaves to sin. We now live under the freedom of God's grace.

2. Gal 4:3,7 NLT. How does Paul describe a life before and after giving their lives to Jesus?

Answer: Before Christ we were slaves to the basic spiritual principles of this world. After Christ we are no longer slaves but God's own – heirs.

3. I Thess 5:6-8 NLT. How should we prepare for the Lord's return?

Answer: We should Stay alert and be clearheaded.

4. 2 Pet 2:19 NLT. What are signs of a false teacher?

Answer: They are slaves of sin and corruption.

Chapter 4

1. Ps 119:65-68 ESV. What and Who does the Psalmist say are good?

Answer: The Psalmist wants to be taught good judgment and knowledge. The Lord is good.

2. John 20:16 ESV. What did Mary call Jesus in Aramaic?

Answer: Rabboni! (Teacher)

3. Jer 9:20 ESV. What did Jeramiah tell the women to do?

Answer: The women were to teach their daughters to lament and a dirge (song of sorrow) to their neighbor.

Chapter 5

1. I Tim 5:14 NIV. Why did Paul encourage the young widows to remarry?

Answer: to give the enemy no opportunity for slander.

2. I John 3:14 NIV. How do we know that we have "passed from death to life"?

Answer: Because we love each other.

3. Prov 22:6 NIV. What are parents to do for their children?

Answer: Start children off on the way they should go

Chapter 6

1. Prov 2:11 NIV. What will discretion do for you?

Answer: Protect you.

2. Acts 9:36 NIV. Who was Tabitha (Dorcas)?

Answer: A disciple from Joppa who was always doing good and helping people.

3. I Tim 5:10 NIV. What are some of the good works that we as Women of God should do?

Answer: "bringing up children, showing hospitality, washing the feet of the Lord's people, helping those in trouble and devoting herself to all kinds of good deeds."

Chapter 7

1. I Cor 6:15 ESV. What are our bodies members of?

Answer: Our bodies are members of Christ

2. I Cor 6:18 ESV. What sin is against one's own body?

Answer: Sexual immorality

3. 2 Cor 11:2 ESV. How did Paul say he presented the Corinthians to Christ?

Answer: as a pure virgin

4. John 4:17-18, 28-29 ESV. How many "husbands" did the Woman at the well say she had? What did she tell the people from her homeland?

Answer: She said she had no husband. She said "Come, see a man who told me all that I ever did. Can this be the Christ?"

Chapter 8

1. Prov 31:27 NIV. What does the Virtuous Woman do regarding her household?

Answer: She watches over the affairs of her household and is not idle

2. Ps 128:3 NIV. How is the wife described by the Psalmist?

Answer: like a fruitful vine within your house

3. I Tim 5:13-14 NIV. What are some of the pitfalls of being idle?

Answer: becoming a busybody saying what should not be said

Chapter 9

1. I Tim 5:9-10 ESV. What were some of the characteristics Paul mentioned of widows in the church?

Answer: Over sixty, faithful to her husband, known for her good deeds, brought up children, showing hospitality and helping others.

2. Ps 34:12-13 ESV. What did the Psalmist say you should do if you want to love life and see good days?

Answer: Keep your tongue from evil and your lips
from speaking deceit.

Chapter 10

1. I Cor 11:3 NIV. How does Paul describe the relationship between the Husband, Wife, and Christ?

Answer: the head of every man is Christ, and the head of the woman is man, and the head of Christ is God.

2. Luke 2:46-51 NIV. How did Jesus respond to Mary and Joseph after he was located at the temple? What can we learn from this?

Answer: He responded by being obedient to them. We can learn to respond properly to authority.

3. Matt 10:30 NIV. God loves you so much my Sister. What does He keep a count of?

Answer: The hairs on your head are numbered.

Chapter 11

1. Luke 22:63-65 NIV. What were some of the wicked things that were done to Christ before His crucifixion?

Answer: Mocked, beat, and said insulting things to the Lord Jesus

2. 2 Pet 2:1-2 NIV. Who will many follow to 'swift destruction'?

Answer: False prophets

3. I Pet 4:4 ESV. Why will the world speak evil of you?

Answer: Because you will not join them in their sinful lifestyle i.e. their "flood of debauchery".

Do You Know Jesus?

Someone may have given you this Bible Study, but you don't know Jesus Christ as your Savior. If that is your situation I want to introduce you to Him right now. It's as simple as John 3:16 where it says, *"For God so loved the world, that he gave his only begotten Son, that whosoever believeth in him should not perish, but have everlasting life."* Jesus offers salvation to you right now, not tomorrow or next week, but right now. Just say this simple prayer.

Father God,
I repent of my sins. I ask Jesus Christ to come into my heart and be my Lord and Savior. I believe that Jesus died on the cross for me. I believe that Jesus rose from the grave, for me. I believe that Jesus is the Son of the Living God. Lord, please help me to live for you and please show me what church I should go to so that I can grow in You Lord. In Jesus' name, Amen.

Author's Social Media

Facebook   www.facebook.com/BelindaLDavis

Instagram   @LadyBella248

YouTube   BEL-DAV TV

Email   sote1989@gmail.com

About the Author

Belinda L. Davis is a Woman of God who has over thirty years of inner-city Ministry experience which involves working with Youth and Young Women. Over her walk with Christ, Belinda has served in many capacities including nine years as a Teen Counsellor at her church. She has also exercised her gift of teaching as a Sunday School and Bible Study Teacher to Youth, Young Adults, and Women.

Belinda is a Prayer Intercessor with Iron Sharpens Iron Ministries which meets weekly with women from around the country to pray about topics of the day. She has founded *Christian Faith Ministries* (CFM) which is focused on ministering to the Detroit and surrounding Communities. One of the arms of CFM is her social media outreach including *Lady B's Women's Bible Study* which can be viewed on her YouTube Channel *BEL-DAV TV*.

Belinda is married to her husband of twenty years, Brian. They live in the Metro Detroit area and attend Macedonia Baptist Church in Detroit where Rev Terry Minor, Sr is their Pastor.

Belinda L. Davis

Notes